365 REASONS YOU'RE THE PERFECT MOM

First published in Great Britain in 2005 by Spruce, an imprint of Octopus Publishing Group Ltd
Carmelite House
50 Victoria Embankment
London EC4Y 0DZ
www.octopusbooks.co.uk

An Hachette UK Company
www.hachette.co.uk

The authorized representative in the EEA is Hachette Ireland, 8 Castlecourt Centre, Dublin 15, D15 XTP3, Ireland
(email: info@hbgi.ie)

This edition was published in 2026

This material was previously published as *1000 Reasons You're the Perfect Mum*

Design copyright © Octopus Publishing Group 2005, 2026
Text copyright © Michael Powell 2005, 2026

Distributed in the US by
Hachette Book Group
1290 Avenue of the Americas,
4th and 5th Floors
New York, NY 10104

Distributed in Canada by
Canadian Manda Group
664 Annette St., Toronto,
Ontario, Canada M6S 2C8

All rights reserved. No part of this work may be reproduced or utilized in any form or by any means, electronic or mechanical, including photocopying, recording or by any information storage and retrieval system, without the prior written permission of the publisher.

Michael Powell asserts the moral right to be identified as the author of this work.

ISBN: 978-1-84181-653-1
eISBN: 978-1-84181-661-6

A CIP catalogue record for this book is available from the British Library.

Printed and bound in China.

10 9 8 7 6 5 4 3 2 1

Publisher: Lucy Pessell
Designers: Isobel Platt & Kathrine Anderson
Senior Editor: Tim Leng
Assistant Editor: Samina Rahman
Production Manager: Allison Gonsalves

365 REASONS YOU'RE THE PERFECT MOM

hamlyn

How often do you make your mother feel uniquely special?

There's a Jewish proverb which says that because God could not be everywhere, he made mothers.

What is motherhood? What is the nature of this unique bond that begins at our birth and guides us throughout our lives? A mother needs patience, courage, tolerance, flexibility, firmness, and a thousand other qualities that grow in the human soul. Above all, she should be a true friend to her child.

At times when our lives seem beset with contradictions and betrayals, a mother's love is the constant that gives us the courage never to quit, the confidence to keep on pursuing our goals, and the conviction that we can reach them.

Our mothers create us. Literally and physically at first, and then mentally and spiritually. We are made from them. And we can never tell them enough what they mean to us.

From time to time, every mother needs to be told that nobody does it better. In many ways it is the least we can do, to say thank you for the infinite sacrifices they've made for us. The hundreds that we know about, and the thousands more that they'll never even tell us about.

If there was any justice in the world, every day would be Mother's Day. We can never do enough to show our gratitude for what they've done for us – but at least we can try.

This book is an attempt to put into words – and to help people find the words, when they need them – the amazing ways which our Mothers have supported us, and made us feel. It is a tribute to mothers and motherhood.

In fact, it's the perfect way to say what every mother wishes to hear.

WHEN YOU COOK, IT IS WITH LOVE.

You never wallow
in the past;
you do not worry
about the future.

YOUR VULNERABLE SIDE DOES NOT PREVENT YOU FROM ACTING WITH CONFIDENCE AND STRENGTH.

YOU ARE STILL MAKING MEMORIES, RATHER THAN LOOKING BACK AT THEM.

Our mothers always remain the strangest, craziest people we've ever met.

MARGUERITE DURAS

YOU HAVE ALWAYS BEEN MUCH MORE TO ME THAN JUST MY MOTHER.

You live for me,
but not through me.

You always manage
to start the day in a
positive frame of mind.

YOU'RE COOL BECAUSE YOU DON'T TRY TO BE.

Of all the rights of women, the greatest is to be a mother.

LIN YUTANG

You believe in your dreams and in doing something about them.

I treasure every gift you have given me for my birthday, even the silly ones.

NO ONE WILL EVER TOUCH MY LIFE EXACTLY THE WAY YOU DO.

WHEN IN DOUBT, YOU CHOOSE HOPE.

You make time to do the things you most desire rather than waste time avoiding those you don't.

SPANISH PROVERB

YOU DISCOVER THE BEST IN PEOPLE BECAUSE YOU LOOK FOR IT.

You are a marvellous mix of serious and silly.

You believe in miracles, but you don't rely on them.

You are a formidable combination of tenderness and toughness.

A mother's love is the fuel that enables a normal human being to do the impossible.

MARION C GARRETTY

THERE WAS NEVER A GREAT MAN WHO HAD NOT A GREAT MOTHER.

You rule your own kingdom.

I WISH I COULD BE STRONG ENOUGH TO DO THE THINGS I HAVE SEEN YOU ACCOMPLISH. BUT BY YOUR EXAMPLE, I HOPE I MIGHT.

You make me feel unique.

Sometimes the strength of motherhood is greater than natural laws.

BARBARA KINGSOLVER

YOU STILL TAKE TIME TO READ, DREAM, AND LOOK AROUND.

If I am lucky enough to be one, I will try to be the sort of parent that I have had.

I DON'T KNOW HOW YOU DID IT, I'M JUST GLAD THAT YOU DID.

You allow your imagination
to decide your future.

**Motherhood: All love
begins and ends there.**

ROBERT BROWNING

I hope that I have inherited
your spiritual DNA.

Even though you have been sitting on the beach longer than me, you still get excited by watching the waves.

THERE IS ALWAYS A SMILE WAITING AT THE CORNERS OF YOUR MOUTH.

NOBODY IS EXACTLY LIKE YOU AND THAT'S WHAT MAKES YOU SO SPECIAL.

I remember my mother's prayers and they have always followed me. They have clung to me all my life.

ABRAHAM LINCOLN

YOU KNOW WHEN TO STAND UP AND SPEAK, AND WHEN TO PUT THE KETTLE ON.

There isn't enough darkness in all the world to snuff out the twinkle in your eye.

**You never let other
people's disapproval
shape your experiences.**

Your love of life has
always been contagious.

**Where there is a mother in
the home, matters go well.**

AMOS BRONSON ALCOTT

You have done so much with your
life that it gives me the confidence
to know that I can do just as much
and even try to do even more.

I LOVE YOUR WONDERFUL CAPACITY FOR DELIGHT.

Motherhood is a flame that once lit can never be extinguished.

WHAT IS MOTHERHOOD? MOTHERHOOD IS GOD'S SPECIAL WAY OF LOVING US THROUGH SOMEONE ELSE.

A mother is she who can take the place of all others but whose place no one else can take.

CARDINAL MERMILLOD

MOTHERHOOD ENTAILS BEING WATCHFUL EVEN WHILE ASLEEP.

Mothers teach us to cherish ourselves and others.

Motherhood has a beginning but no end.

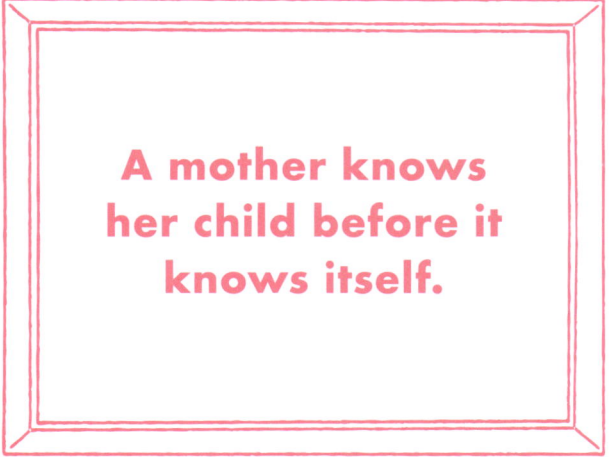

A mother knows her child before it knows itself.

To describe my mother would be to write about a hurricane in its perfect power.

MAYA ANGELOU

MOTHERS COME WITH A LIFETIME GUARANTEE.

A mother never asks, "What's in it for me?"

MOTHERHOOD IS AN ETERNAL EMBRACE.

MOTHERS ARE THE BEST MEDICINE.

There is no way to be a perfect mother but a million ways to be a good one.

JILL CHURCHILL

A MOTHER IS LIKE THE SUN – YOU CAN FEEL HER WARMTH EVEN WHEN SHE IS FAR AWAY.

MOTHERS HOLD THEIR CHILDREN'S HANDS FOR ONLY A SHORT WHILE, BUT CLASP THEIR HEARTS FOREVER.

A mother is the inspiration for all acts of creation.

Thanks to my mother, not a single cardboard box has found its way back into society. We receive gifts in boxes from stores that went out of business years ago.

ERMA BOMBECK

Mothers are always at the end of the phone, with words of wisdom, if things go wrong.

A mother's love is a gift that never stops giving.

A mother is like a soft cushion that breaks every fall.

> **A MOTHER ALWAYS REMINDS US OF WHO WE ARE AND WHERE WE COME FROM.**

A mother is a person who, seeing there are only four pieces of pie for five people, promptly announces she never did care for pie.

TENNEVA JORDAN

THOUGH EVERYONE HAS A MOTHER, EACH IS STILL A RARE TREASURE.

A mother must tread the line between mothering her child, and being their friend, with great care.

A MOTHER'S LOVE IS
RARELY EARNED
BUT FREELY GIVEN.

MOTHERHOOD IS A PRICELESS TREASURE THAT CAN ONLY BE CHERISHED.

**A mother is a mother still,
The holiest thing alive.**

SAMUEL TAYLOR COLERIDGE

A MOTHER IS A SHELTERING TREE IN A STRANGE FOREST.

A mother's eyesight becomes a little less sharp when she looks for faults in her own child.

Love is a sonnet, but a mother's love is an epic poem.

SOMETIMES A MOTHER IS ALL YOU HAVE AND ALL YOU NEED.

The mother's heart is the child's schoolroom.

HENRY WARD BEECHER

Mothers care so deeply that they aren't ashamed to make it public.

A MOTHER'S SHOULDERS CAN CARRY THE WEIGHT OF THE WORLD, YET HER ARMS ARE GENTLE ENOUGH TO GIVE COMFORT.

Imagine a world without mothers – it would be like a world without water.

MOTHERS SPEAK LOUDER THAN WORDS.

Mother is the name for God in the lips and hearts of little children.

WILLIAM MAKEPEACE THACKERAY

EVERYTHING STARTS WITH A MOTHER.

Our mothers are both the door by which we enter this world, and its key.

A mother is a gift that gives itself to you.

MONEY MIGHT MAKE US WEALTHY, BUT A MOTHER'S LOVE MAKES US RICH.

There is no velvet so soft as a mother's lap, no rose as lovely as her smile, no path so flowery as that imprinted with her footsteps.

ARCHIBALD THOMPSON

A MOTHER'S PRAISE IS WORTH A THOUSAND TIMES MORE THAN PRAISE COMING FROM OTHERS.

MOTHERHOOD BEGINS AT HOME AND NEVER ENDS.

No act of motherhood, no matter how small, is ever wasted.

A MOTHER'S LOVE COMES AND GROWS, NEVER EBBS AND ALWAYS FLOWS.

No language can express the power and beauty and heroism of a mother's love.

EDWIN HUBBELL CHAPIN

MOTHER: A NOUN, BUT MAINLY A VERB.

You listen to everything I say before you ask questions or make a comment.

A MOTHER CAN SAY WITH A SMILE EVERYTHING YOU WISH TO HEAR.

A MOTHER'S AFFECTION IS UNWAVERING – A CANDLE'S FLAME THAT DOESN'T FLICKER EVEN IN A STORM.

Together we can see through all the darkness.

A mother's arms are made of tenderness and children sleep soundly in them.

VICTOR HUGO

A MOTHER IS OFTEN REQUIRED TO WATCH HER CHILDREN FROM A SAFE DISTANCE, WHEN SHE WOULD RATHER COVER HER EYES.

REMEMBER THAT MOTHERHOOD IS A BEGINNING, NOT A DESTINATION.

Motherhood is an ocean of rapture: so long as you can sail through the storms.

We have but one mother,
but life will offer a
thousand imitations.

Some are kissing mothers and some are scolding mothers, but it is love just the same – and most mothers kiss and scold together.

PEARL S BUCK

A WOMAN WHO BELIEVES IN HERSELF CAN DELIGHT IN MOTHERHOOD.

Motherhood is an opportunity to make the world a better place, without having to wait for the world to change.

MOTHERS ARE PROOF THAT MAGIC EXISTS.

There is no 'I' in 'mother.'

It is not easy being a mother. If it were easy, fathers would do it.

BEA ARTHUR

YOUR LOVE IS BIGGER THAN ANYTHING THAT CAN HAPPEN TO ME.

Setting off on my journey through life, it's you who've made sure I've packed enough sweaters.

YOU ARE STRONG BUT SOFT IN THE WAY YOU LOVE ME.

JUST BY YOUR PRESENCE, YOU HAVE CHANGED THE WORLD AROUND ME.

Who ran to help me when I fell,
And would some pretty story tell,
Or kiss the place to make it well?
My Mother.

JANE TAYLOR

THANK YOU FOR ALL THE TIMES YOU HAVE SPONTANEOUSLY TOLD ME, "I LOVE YOU."

Because you have made me feel so secure, I can accomplish great things because I no longer seek security.

Walking with you through the clouds is better than walking alone under a blue sky.

YOU ARE THE BUD FROM WHICH MY HAPPINESS BLOSSOMS.

> No language can express the power and beauty and heroism of a mother's love.
>
> EDWIN CHAPIN

BEING DEEPLY LOVED BY YOU GIVES ME STRENGTH.

You never make a big deal out of anything, except me.

You find your happiness along the way, not at the end of the journey.

At times when I feel all alone I think of you, and my heart heads home.

When sadness intrudes and spirits sag, you offer guidance and strength.

MOTHERS FEED THEIR CHILD'S BODY AND SOUL: THEY ALWAYS PREPARE A BANQUET WHEN YOU ASK FOR A SNACK.

The art of mothering is to teach the art of living to children.

ELAINE HEFFNER

SOMETIMES, JUST SOMETIMES, YOU ARE A PUSHOVER – AND THAT'S NICE.

You have taught me the meaning of 'unconditional love.'

YOU INVEST THE LOVE THAT I GIVE YOU AND RETURN IT WITH INTEREST.

Every day you have brought me simple pleasures out of which I have been able to make some wonderful memories.

All that I am or ever hope to be,
I owe to my angel Mother.

ABRAHAM LINCOLN

I have lost count of the times you have looked me in the eye and told me how special I am.

You have always encouraged me to step forward into growth rather than step back into safety.

YOU ARE GENTLE WITH YOURSELF SO THAT YOU CAN BE GENTLE WITH OTHERS.

YOU SHELTERED ME UNDER YOUR WINGS WHILE I WAS LEARNING TO USE MY OWN.

The first great gift we can bestow on others is a good example.

THOMAS MORELL

THE ONLY TIME YOU EVER GET IN MY WAY IS WHEN YOU CATCH ME AS I FALL.

YOU SEE LOVE EVERYWHERE BECAUSE IT SURROUNDS YOU.

My childhood was like a clear blue sky – a memory that I carry with me and bring out whenever clouds are obscuring the sun.

YOU NEVER UNDERESTIMATE THE POWER OF LOVE.

Motherhood is an act of endless forgiveness.

My mother was the most beautiful woman I ever saw. All I am I owe to my mother. I attribute all my success in life to the moral, intellectual, and physical education I received from her.

GEORGE WASHINGTON

YOU HELP ME TO HELP MYSELF TO HAPPINESS.

It gives me strength to know that someone loves me whatever I do.

If I know what love is, it's because of you.

YOU LOVE ME

IN SPITE OF MYSELF.

My heart will never outgrow you.

Mama was my greatest teacher, a teacher of compassion, love, and fearlessness. If love is sweet as a flower, then my mother is that sweet flower of love.

STEVIE WONDER

YOUR LOVE HAS PROVED THAT WHAT I AM IS MORE THAN GOOD ENOUGH.

You keep me safe in your prayers, heal me with your love, and nourish me with your laughter.

WHEN I DESERVE IT THE LEAST, YOU LOVE ME THE MOST.

You can see star quality in me, even when to my eyes, the skies are cloudy.

Men are what their mothers made them.

RALPH WALDO EMERSON

Two of the most dynamic forces in my life are your love and support.

Every time I have tested your patience, you have passed the test.

I'LL NEVER BE

TOO OLD FOR

ONE OF YOUR HUGS.

WHEN PEOPLE REMARK THAT I TAKE AFTER YOU, I AM FLATTERED.

Children require guidance and sympathy far more than instruction.
ANNIE SULLIVAN

THANK YOU FOR STANDING ON THE SIDELINES AND CHEERING ME ON.

You give me the ability to soar.

Wherever I am, it is you that underpins my universe.

Side by side or miles apart, you are always close to my heart.

The tie which links mother and child is of such pure and immaculate strength as to be never violated.

WASHINGTON IRVING

You have always tried to build a world around me.

I am like a favourite poem to you. You may not always understand me, but you will always love me.

You make me think before I react because you have my best interests at heart.

IF MOTHERS WERE FLOWERS, I'D STILL PICK YOU.

From a scraped knee to a broken heart – you can cure anything.

LIKE A STAR, YOU SEEM TO SHINE BRIGHTEST WHEN THE NIGHT IS AT ITS DARKEST.

When I became a mother, something inside me shifted...it took the focus off me and put it on something much more important.

GILLIAN ANDERSON

Life is sometimes a struggle, but your steadfast love gives me the confidence to hang tough.

YOU CAN TOUCH MY HEART FROM ACROSS THE WORLD OR ACROSS THE ROOM.

What do girls do who haven't any mothers to help them through their troubles?

LOUISA MAY ALCOTT

At times you don't know where I'm going, but the power of your love lights the way ahead.

ALL THROUGH MY LIFE, YOU HAVE SCATTERED BLESSINGS.

You've always driven me everywhere I need to go – even when I drove you crazy.

I hope that one day you will be able to rely on me as much as I have relied on you.

You never get over bein' a child long's you have a mother to go to.

SARAH ORNE JEWETT

When my heart has been hurt, you teach me to love again.

YOU KNOW WHEN TO HUG ME AND TELL ME THAT IT WILL ALL COME GOOD.

YOU HAVE TAUGHT ME THAT PEOPLE ALWAYS COME FIRST.

I grew in you, but I can see that a part of you has grown in me.

I shall never forget my mother; for it was she who planted and nurtured the first seeds of good within me.

IMMANUEL KANT

WHEN TIMES ARE HARD, YOU KEEP YOUR HEART SOFT.

When my dreams turn to dust, you sweep up the mess.

YOU ARE THE ROCK UNDER MY FEET THAT KEEPS ME STANDING WHEN ALL MY OTHER SUPPORTS HAVE FALLEN AWAY.

You've taught me to think big thoughts but cherish small pleasures.

Youth fades; love droops; the leaves of friendship fall;
A mother's secret hope outlives them all.

OLIVER WENDELL HOLMES

YOU REMIND ME THAT IT'S NEVER TOO LATE TO LEARN SOMETHING NEW.

YOU GO OUT OF YOUR WAY TO KEEP ME ON THE RIGHT PATH.

I have learned from you never to wait for other people's permission to be extraordinary.

YOU BELIEVE THERE IS ALWAYS MORE LIFE TO BE DISCOVERED.

A mother is not a person to lean on, but a person to make leaning unnecessary.

DOROTHY CANFIELD FISHER

Your attitude has made all the difference.

WITHOUT YOU, EVERYTHING IN MY LIFE WOULD SEEM SMALLER.

I AM TODAY WHERE YOUR LESSONS HAVE BROUGHT ME; I WILL BE TOMORROW WHEREVER YOUR LESSONS WILL TAKE ME.

Thank you for equipping me with the tools to design my own happiness.

Only mothers can think of the future– because they give birth to it in their children.

MAXIM GORKY

You have advised me never to be satisfied with success or discouraged by failure.

You constantly encourage me to abandon mere satisfaction in favour of true happiness.

LIFE IS A SERIES OF PATHS: SOME OF THOSE I CHOOSE HAVE ALREADY BEEN TRAVELLED BY YOU FOR A GREATER DISTANCE; UNTRIED PATHS AWAIT US BOTH.

YOU ALWAYS ADJUST MY SAILS TO CATCH THE WIND.

Mother – that was the bank where we deposited all our hurts and worries.

T DEWITT TALMAGE

YOU TAKE MY HAND AND LEAD ME INTO THE HERE AND NOW.

YOU SET BOUNDARIES, BUT NOT LIMITS.

You have demonstrated to me both the value and the price of being prepared.

You have taught me so many things I thought I already knew.

My mother had a slender, small body, but a large heart – a heart so large that everybody's joys found welcome in it, and hospitable accommodation.

MARK TWAIN

> THE POINT OF YOUR LIFE HAS BEEN TO SHOW ME HOW TO LIVE THE WAY I REALLY WANT TO LIVE.

> You encourage me to make opportunities more than take chances.

I HAVE LEARNED FROM YOU THAT SOMETIMES RAINBOWS ARE THERE TO BE CHASED.

Thank you for reminding me that I am never finished.

If you bungle raising your children, I don't think whatever else you do well matters very much.

JACQUELINE KENNEDY ONASSIS

YOU HELP ME TO WALK CONFIDENTLY IN THE DIRECTION OF MY DREAMS.

You are the window through which I first viewed the world.

YOU HAVE HELPED ME TO RECOGNIZE THE BLESSING HIDDEN IN EVERY OBSTACLE.

More than teaching me, you have filled me with the wish to learn.

Biology is the least of what makes someone a mother.

OPRAH WINFREY

You know the right moment to step in and say, "Let me do it for you."

You have given me the strength to help others and the support to be myself.

SOMETIMES, YOU JOLT ME OUT OF MY COMFORT ZONE.

YOU DIDN'T JUST RAISE ME, YOU RAISED THE BAR.

For that's what a woman, a mother, wants – to teach her children to take an interest in life. She knows it's safer for them to be interested in other people's happiness than to believe in their own.

MARGUERITE DURAS

YOU HELP ME TO FULFILL SOME OF MY DESIRES AND LET GO OF THE ONES THAT ARE NOT WORTH FOLLOWING.

I know that life will keep on getting better if I follow your example.

You have raised me to believe that there really is good in the world.

You have always worked, not just wished, for what you want.

The heart of a mother is a deep abyss at the bottom of which you will always find forgiveness.

HONORÉ DE BALZAC

YOU HAVE NO REGRETS, AND THAT IS A GREAT EXAMPLE FOR ME TO FOLLOW.

You are living proof that being playful, rebellious, and immature has its strengths.

If motherhood is a voyage that a woman maps out as she goes along, how come you always had such a good idea of where you were going?

When faced with a tough decision I always ask myself, "What would my mother do here?"

My mother's love for me was so great I have worked hard to justify it.

MARC CHAGALL

YOU HAVE NEVER FOUGHT MY BATTLES, BUT YOU HAVE ENCOURAGED ME TO STAND UP FOR MYSELF.

You demand so little from me, and give so much.

When my life is too busy, you help to slow me down.

INSTEAD OF POINTING A FINGER, YOU HOLD OUT YOUR HAND.

The world is full of women blindsided by the unceasing demands of motherhood, still flabbergasted by how a job can be terrific and torturous.

ANNA QUINDLEN

THANK YOU FOR HELPING ME SEARCH FOR THE RIGHT KIND OF LIFE.

You can speak two languages: one of them is hope and the other is trust.

You have shown that I can live happily ever after, so long as I take one day at a time.

YOU KNOW WHEN TO HOLD ON AND WHEN TO LET GO.

A mother is neither cocky, nor proud, because she knows the school principal may call at any minute to report that her child has just driven a motorcycle through the gymnasium.

MARY KAY BLAKELY

When my life unravels, you stitch me together again.

YOU CAN SEE THE MIRACLES IN ME THAT ARE INVISIBLE TO OTHERS.

> You believed in me and never gave up.

FROM YOU I LEARNED THE SKILL OF TRUSTING OTHERS.

Motherhood has a very humanizing effect. Everything gets reduced to essentials.

MERYL STREEP

My safety net is woven from the threads of your belief.

Thank you for giving me the freedom to make mistakes.

I can rely on you to stay calm when things are a mess.

Even when I fail, you trust me to learn from my mistakes.

Because I am a mother, I am capable of being shocked: as I never was when I was not one.

MARGARET ATWOOD

YOU BELIEVE IN ME ALL THE WAY – AND BACK.

> You have made me appreciative of myself by appreciating me.

YOU MAY BE A BIT SQUARE, BUT I LOVE HAVING YOU AROUND.

YOU BROUGHT ME UP AND YOU NEVER BRING ME DOWN.

Motherhood is the strangest thing, it can be like being one's own Trojan horse.

REBECCA WEST

You manage to see me as I am rather than as you want me to be.

You praise the ordinary and celebrate the exceptional.

You have always rejoiced in me for my own sake.

WHEN I TRY TO CLIMB MOUNTAINS, YOU DON'T TELL ME IT IS IMPOSSIBLE; INSTEAD YOU ASK ME TO WAVE WHEN I REACH THE TOP.

Mother's love is peace.
It need not be acquired,
it need not be deserved.

ERICH FROMM

YOU LISTEN WITHOUT JUDGEMENT AND PRAISE WITHOUT QUALIFICATION.

YOU HAVE ALWAYS TRIED TO SEE THE WORLD FROM MY POINT OF VIEW.

YOUR LOVE ISN'T BLIND; IT JUST SEES WHAT MATTERS.

You have taught me to be patient with myself.

A mother's love for her child is like nothing else in the world. It knows no law, no pity, it dares all things and crushes down remorselessly all that stands in its path.

AGATHA CHRISTIE

YOU NEVER ALLOW ME TO THINK LESS OF MYSELF.

WHILE OTHERS COMPLICATE THEIR LIVES, YOU BUSY YOURSELF WITH ENJOYING YOURS.

My heart beats easier when you are near.

A mother understands what a child does not say.

JEWISH PROVERB

> With you I can totally be myself.

YOU ACCEPT ALL OF ME.

YOU DON'T EXPECT ME TO BE GOOD AT EVERYTHING, BUT YOU DO ENCOURAGE AMAZING RESULTS.

You know how to be yourself, but you never try to tell others how they ought to be.

YOU ALWAYS FIND SOMETHING TO BE THANKFUL FOR.

YOU HELP ME TO SEE THE FUN IN TRYING TO DO THE IMPOSSIBLE.

The hand that rocks the cradle is the hand that rules the world.

W S ROSS

You appreciate the unusual, but you celebrate the ordinary too.

You shared my past, believe in my future, and accept me today for who I am.

YOU HELP ME TO BE THANKFUL FOR THE WAY THINGS ARE.

You remind me to pause
and just be happy.

**Life began with waking up
and loving my mother's face.**

GEORGE ELIOT

YOU HAVE ALWAYS TRIED
TO LIVE GRACEFULLY.

YOU HELP ME TO TAKE MY LIFE LESS SERIOUSLY.

In life, when those around you are singing off-key, you don't cover your ears.

You try never to underrate anyone's intelligence, least of all your own.

Women know
The way to rear up children (to be just),
They know a simple, merry, tender knack
Of tying sashes, fitting baby-shoes,
And stringing pretty words
that make no sense,
And kissing full sense into empty words.

ELIZABETH BARRETT BROWNING

IF I HAD TO CHOOSE ALL THE QUALITIES FOR A GOOD MOTHER, IT WOULD BE THOSE I FIND IN YOU.

No challenge is too big for you, no problem too small.

THE THINGS THAT YOU FEAR, YOU SEEK TO UNDERSTAND.

You always give me your blessing, even though you are the one person from whom I do not feel the need to seek it.

Anyone who doesn't miss the past never had a mother.

GREGORY NUNN

I ALWAYS WANT TO TRY HARDER EVEN THOUGH I KNOW THAT YOU'LL STILL BE PROUD OF ME WHATEVER THE RESULTS.

Thank you for helping me go beyond my limits.

BEFORE EXPRESSING AN OPINION, YOU TRY TO UNDERSTAND THOSE OF OTHERS.

I can make a fool of myself and you're still proud of me for trying.

> You have nothing to prove to me.

Sometimes the laughter in mothering is the recognition of the ironies and absurdities. Sometimes, though, it's just pure, unthinking delight.

BARBARA SCHAPIRO

YOU HAVE NEVER BEEN SILENT ABOUT THE THINGS THAT MATTER.

How do you manage to be soft and tough at the same time?

WHENEVER YOU GET THE OPPORTUNITY TO SAY A KIND WORD, YOU TAKE IT.

**My mother is a poem
I'll never be able to write,
though everything I write
is a poem to my mother.**

SHARON DOUBIAGO

YOU LISTEN TO ME WITH SOFTNESS IN YOUR EYES.

You never say, "I told you so!" – even if you did!

With your help I can face life as I truly am, and not worry about what others think.

You manage to be both a student and a teacher.

**That best academy,
a mother's knee.**

JAMES RUSSELL LOWELL

YOU TAUGHT ME TO SING THE SONG OF LIFE – AND NOW I'M COMPOSING MY OWN TUNE.

While others agonize, you organize.

JUST THE THOUGHT OF YOU BRINGS ME COMFORT ON DIFFICULT DAYS.

YOU CLOTHED ME IN EMOTIONAL SUPPORT – AND CLOTHES, OF COURSE.

My mother's gifts of courage to me were both large and small. The latter are woven so subtly into the fabric of my psyche that I can hardly distinguish where she stops and I begin.

MAYA ANGELOU

Somehow you can always tell when something is wrong with me, even though I have a big smile on my face.

> You know me better than I know myself.

YOU NEVER LOSE THE PLOT, BECAUSE YOU ARE WRITING THE STORY.

You make me believe that
I deserve what I want.

**You may have tangible wealth untold;
Caskets of jewels and coffers of gold.
Richer than I you can never be –
I had a mother who read to me.**

STRICKLAND GILLILAN

YOU SIMPLY PAY ATTENTION TO ME, AND THAT IS ENOUGH.

YOU REPEAT THE SAME OLD STORIES, AND I MIGHT GROAN, BUT I SECRETLY LOVE TO HEAR THEM.

You always listen to what I don't say.

THE GREATEST GIFT YOU HAVE GIVEN ME IS YOUR LISTENING HEART.

Most mothers are instinctive philosophers.

HARRIET BEECHER STOWE

THANK YOU FOR TELLING ME STORIES DURING THUNDERSTORMS. I NEVER KNEW THAT YOU WERE SCARED, TOO.

You refuse to keep silent about the things that matter.

You always keep lines of communication open, even in frosty conditions.

YOU ALWAYS HAVE THE COURAGE TO TELL ME WHAT I NEED TO HEAR.

Intense love does not measure, it just gives.

MOTHER TERESA

Before passing judgement, you listen a thousand times.

YOU NEVER LET ME DOWN – EXCEPT WHEN I'M OVERINFLATED.

You take from others only those things which you yourself are willing to give.

YOU HAVE GIVEN ME TWO LIVES: MINE AND YOURS.

God could not be everywhere and therefore he made mothers.

JEWISH PROVERB

Thank you for giving me something only you could give – yourself.

Sometimes you are the wind in my sails, and sometimes you are the calm in the eye of the storm.

I AM WHAT I AM TODAY BECAUSE OF THE CHOICES YOU MADE YESTERDAY.

You share your blessings, instead of hoarding them.

YOU NEVER IGNORE ANOTHER PERSON'S DISTRESS.

By and large, mothers and housewives are the only workers who do not have regular time off. They are the great vacationless class.

ANNE MORROW LINDBERGH

YOU HAVE TAUGHT ME THAT I CAN AND DO MAKE A DIFFERENCE.

When my heart is breaking, you get baking.

YOU HAVE HELPED ME TO VIEW CHANGE AS AN ADVENTURE.

You have shown me how to give of myself.

A man never sees all that his mother has been to him until it's too late to let her know he sees it.

WILLIAM DEAN HOWELLS

EVEN THOUGH I CAN NEVER REPAY YOU, YOU KEEP GIVING.

YOU ALWAYS PUT FAMILY FIRST.

For you, there is a big gap between 'good' and 'good enough'.

THE WORLD IS YOUR KINDERGARTEN. THANKS FOR INVITING ME TO PLAY.

> A mother who is really a mother is never free.
>
> HONORÉ DE BALZAC

THANKS FOR BEING HERE – WHEN THE WHOLE WORLD WAS OVER THERE.

You have always given
me a generous handful
of second chances.

It will take a lifetime of
living my life the way
you showed me, to thank
you for showing me.

**YOU NEVER GIVE AS GOOD AS
YOU GET – YOU GIVE BETTER.**

THE WORLD OFFERS ITSELF TO ME BECAUSE YOU OFFERED YOURSELF FIRST.

YOU HAVE WOVEN STRENGTH, COLOUR, AND SPARKLE INTO THE FABRIC OF MY LIFE.

Making the decision to have a child – it's momentous. It is to decide forever to have your heart go walking around outside your body.

ELIZABETH STONE

When you ask me a question, it makes me think.

YOU SAVE ALL THE BEST BITS FOR ME.

You give help and comfort first, before you ever think of giving advice.

You always believe you could have done more for me: you couldn't have.

YOU HAVE SPREAD YOUR DREAMS UNDER MY FEET.

When I need a helping hand, you never need to ask if there's anything you can do. You just do it.

You have shown me that taking part in a race is more important than trying to reach the finishing line first.

You made sacrifices so that I could follow my dreams.

Whenever I give you a gift, you always act like it is the best thing in the world.

IN TIMES OF PROSPERITY YOU ARE THERE; IN TIMES OF ADVERSITY YOU ARE HERE.

The watchful mother tarries nigh, though sleep has closed her infant's eyes.

JOHN KEBLE

A mother is the truest friend we have, when trials, heavy and sudden, fall upon us; when adversity takes the place of prosperity; when friends, who rejoice with us in our sunshine, desert us; when troubles thicken around us, still will she cling to us, and endeavour by her kind precepts and counsels to dissipate the clouds of darkness, and cause peace to return to our hearts.

WASHINGTON IRVING